uick
&
easy

Saltwater Aquarium Setup & Care

Quick & Easy Saltwater Aquarium Setup & Care

Project Team
Editor: Brian M. Scott
Copy Editor: Stephanie Hays
Design: Patricia Escabi
Series Design: Mary Ann Kahn

T.F.H. Publications
President/CEO: Glen S. Axelrod
Executive Vice President: Mark E. Johnson
Publisher: Christopher T. Reggio
Production Manager: Kathy Bontz

T.F.H. Publications, Inc.
One TFH Plaza
Third and Union Avenues
Neptune City, NJ 07753

05 06 07 08 09 1 3 5 7 9 8 6 4 2

Library of Congress Cataloging-in-Publication Data
Quick & easy saltwater aquarium setup and care / TFH staff.
p. cm.
Includes index.
ISBN 0-7938-1043-4 (alk. paper)
1. Marine aquariums. I. Title: Quick and easy saltwater aquarium setup and
care. II. T.F.H. Publications, Inc.
SF457.1Q85 2005
639.34'2–dc22
2005011903

This book has been published with the intent to provide accurate and authoritative information
in regard to the subject matter within. While every precaution has been taken in preparation of
this book, the author and publisher expressly disclaim responsibility for any errors, omissions, or
adverse effects arising from the use or application of the information contained herein. The techniques and suggestions are used at the reader's discretion and are not to be considered a sub-
stitute for veterinary care. If you suspect a medical problem, consult your veterinarian.

The Leader In Responsible Animal Care For Over 50 Years!™
www.tfhpublications.com

Table
of Contents

Introduction to the Saltwater Aquarium

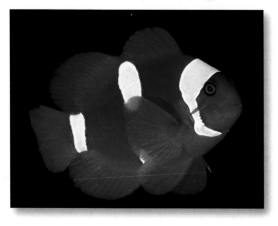

Perhaps you've been captivated by the impossibly colored fishes in your dealer's tanks, or maybe you've gained confidence in your aquaristic skills with a few freshwater tanks and are looking forward to the challenge of a saltwater one. Then again, maybe those tanks you've been passing up for years, with the reasoning that you could buy a whole tank full of tetras for the price of one saltwater fish, might now show individual prices that aren't all that different from some rare or unique freshwater fishes. Perhaps since you've kept some mollies or scats or some other brackish water inhabitants, you now realize that the dividing line between freshwater and saltwater fishes is not as clear as you may have been led to believe. Whatever your reason for considering a marine aquarium, you could not have picked a better time to start one.

First of all, the saltwater hobby, once reserved to the elite few who had mastered the chemistry and had the tenacity and the financial means needed to pursue this branch of the aquarium hobby, is now open to virtually anyone interested in it. While it appears that some marine aquarists spend more time measuring redox potentials and monitoring ion concentrations than they do watching their fishes, it is possible, thanks to that same modern technology, to set up a marine tank that is fairly simple to maintain. And because of the increased interest in the keeping of marine fishes, there are now many inexpensive products available for the hobbyist that were previously unobtainable at any price just a few years ago.

Additionally, the price of many marine fishes is now much more within reach of the average hobbyist. The concern about reef-damaging cyanide trapping, plus improved methods of shipping and handling fish, have resulted in lower mortality rates, which of course means lower prices. It is very easy to get hooked when you visit a pet shop that has some freshwater cichlids bearing higher prices than the fishes in a tank of assorted saltwater damselfishes, for example.

The maintenance of an invertebrate reef aquarium is right now at the cutting edge of marine technology, and it is rightly the domain of knowledgeable, experienced hobbyists. However, the trickledown of expertise and products that enable the captive reproduction of a microcosm of a tropical coral reef full of invertebrates has also given the marine fish hobby a wealth of knowledge and equipment to simplify and enhance the keeping of marine vertebrates as well.

Taking the Plunge

Are you ready for salt water? You're taking the right first step in reading books like this one and getting the information you need to

Maintaining a beautiful reef aquarium like this one is rightly the domain of knowledgeable, experienced hobbyists.

make your initial foray into the marine hobby a successful one. If you have the desire and are willing to arm yourself with practical knowledge before you set up that tank, you are likely not only to succeed in keeping such a challenging and rewarding aquarium but also to go on to increase your marine tank space.

All of the experience you may have gained with freshwater tanks will carry over into saltwater tanks. Granted, a few things, like salt mixes and specific gravity, are not part of the freshwater hobby, but all of the basic principles of freshwater aquarium management exist for marine husbandry as well. In the following chapters, we will discuss setting up your first marine tank.

We will be talking about establishing a very simple and inexpensive marine collection. Just as you slowly got your feet wet with freshwater fishes, you should start out slowly with saltwater fishes. You can save the more difficult species for later on, but you won't be sacrificing the excitement of a marine tank, nor will you have to forgo the sparkling beauty, as many of the hardiest and least expensive marine fishes are among the most colorful.

Introduction to the Saltwater Aquarium 7

Let thriving aquariums be an inspiration to you, not an impossible goal.

Befriend a Dealer

From the very beginning, one of the best resources you can have is a knowledgeable, helpful tropical fish dealer. He or she can provide you with sound advice, help with problems, and a selection of high-quality fish. Your dealer should be able to tell you a great deal about all of the products and procedures, and he or she should be able to tell you what you need now and what is best kept for later. Dealers who believe that the best way to succeed is to inform their customers and to sell them only what the customers actually need will not have you waste your money on useless gadgets or talk you into buying products beyond the scope of your initial attempt at salt water. They will also refrain from selling you incompatible fishes, fishes that won't eat, or fishes that won't live out the week. These are the types of services that make pet shops and aquarium stores the most popular outlets for purchasing quality marine livestock and equipment.

Aquarium
Selection

Years ago, when the lack of knowledge and technology made everything concerning the marine hobby difficult, the best salt water to be had was carried from the beach in a bucket, and people had rows of black and white marbled tanks punctuated by an occasional shiny-new stainless steel one. The first advice to the beginner back then was about using only stainless steel tanks for salt water and of coating all exposed metal with epoxy to keep it from contacting and reacting with the salty spray. Today, with precisely engineered artificial salt mixes and the ubiquitous all-glass aquarium, the first advice to prospective marine aquarists usually centers on the size of the tank.

While it is true for both freshwater and saltwater tanks that the larger the aquarium, the more forgiving it (and its inhabitants) will be of mistakes you make, for marine tanks it is doubly so. The natural marine environment is a much more complex and stable one than freshwater lakes and streams. The marine aquarium, on the other hand, is potentially a terribly unstable environment, one lacking in many of the natural buffers and controls that, while adding to its complexity, also preserve a safe, hospitable, unchanging environment for its inhabitants. Therefore, when we're talking about saltwater tanks, instead of thinking the bigger, the better, think the biggest, the best.

A Beginner's Aquarium

The absolute minimum aquarium that is recommended for a beginner is a 30-gallon (114 l) aquarium, and a 50-gallon (190 l) or more would be preferable. This is not to say that even the smallest aquaria cannot be used for marine setups. However, it is recommended that these "micro-systems" only be attempted by the more experienced saltwater hobbyists. Even if it seems counterintuitive to you, it's true that the larger the tank, the simpler its care—and the easier time you will have of it.

Placing tangs in the beginner's aquarium is probably not a good idea, because they are sometimes aggressive and hard to acclimate properly.

The extremely popular 48-inch-long 55-gallon (209 l) aquarium is a good choice for beginners, and these tanks are often available in a special package deal with full hood and reflector at a most reasonable cost. Such a tank is large enough to give you some leeway until your husbandry comes up to speed. In addition, marine fishes must be stocked at rates considerably lower than those for their freshwater cousins, and many beginners can't bring themselves to keep a tank with only four or five fish in it. The 55-gallon (209 l) tank lets you have a little more variety and still stay within safe limits.

It's Up To You

There is nothing "wrong" about any size or shape aquarium. As long as the constraints of the tank are understood, you can select any tank you want, but you must concern yourself with the surface area and respect the limitations of the tank you choose.

The popularity of this tank stems from its proportions for viewing the aquarium contents. Unfortunately, the tall, thin design, so aesthetically pleasing, is not in the best interest of the tank's inhabitants. The factor that determines the carrying capacity, or stocking rate, of an aquarium, all other things being equal, is not the volume of the water that it holds but rather its overall surface area, since that is where the gas exchange takes place. The absolute volume of water is a factor in the ability of the tank to accommodate pollutants and store oxygen, but only for an extremely limited time. It is foolhardy to rely on mere volume to preserve water quality, since the "size" of an aquarium depends on how you measure it.

Importance of Surface Area to Volume

For example, the 4-foot-long (120 cm) 55-gallon (209 l) tank has a surface area of about 4 square feet. The squatter 3-foot-long (90 cm) 50-gallon (190 l) aquarium, on the other hand, has a surface area of about 4-square feet, so the "smaller" (in gallons or length) tank is actually "larger" in surface area! A 75-gallon (284 l) tank, with the same front glass dimensions and viewing area as a 55-gallon (209 l), has a surface area of about 6 square feet, a 50% increase over the 55-gallon (209 l), but this is the same surface area as a 90-gallon tank (341 l), which is simply taller.

Aquarium Placement

As with any other setup, the tank must be placed on a solid, level surface, preferably on a commercially built stand designed for the particular tank you have. A 55-gallon (209 l) aquarium full of water will weigh in at around 600 pounds (274 kg), so you have to be sure the floor you place it on can take the strain. Stands with four solid sides rather than a top rim and legs are preferable in this regard because should the tank's weight be supported by four legs with 1-inch diameter feet, then the total weight is borne by just over 3 square inches of floor, for a pressure of almost 200 pounds (91.5 kg) per square inch for a 600-pound (274 kg) load. The same load, borne by a continuous perimeter rim goes down to nearly 7 pounds per square inch.

The tank should be away from temperature extremes such as doors, windows, heating and cooling vents, etc., and it should be situated where you can enjoy and service it as you go about your daily routine.

Proximity to a drain and faucet for water changes and a ground fault protected electrical supply should also figure into your choice of location for the tank. That last is important enough to stress by repeating that you wouldd never use your hair dryer in the shower. Well, you should never plug any aquarium appliance into any outlet that is not protected by either a ground fault interrupting (GFI) receptacle or a circuit covered by a GFI circuit breaker.

Outfitting Your Saltwater Aquarium

Now that you know a little bit more about tank selection and the importance of the surface area to volume ratio, let's look at what it will take—equipment-wise—to outfit your new marine aquarium. The first place that we'll start is with the water itself. Believe it or not, salt water is not just some water and salt mixed together. It's a specially blended mixture of water, salts, trace elements, and other very important ingredients. Let's have a look.

Understanding Salt Water

Obviously, the water you use in a marine tank will be salty, but how do you get it that way? If you're used to hatching brine shrimp, you may wonder if you could just throw some kosher or solar salt into the tank. If you live on a coast, you may imagine how much money you will save by using ocean water for free instead of buying salt mixes, and even if you've already decided to use salt mixes, you are probably wondering which one to use and whether that really makes a difference. Let's consider these one at a time.

Now, while you beach dwellers might think that natural is the simplest and least expensive way to go, you should reconsider. Unless you are reading this on some pristine uncharted Pacific island, the water along the coast is often polluted. All of the chemical and physical debris that mankind dumps into the ocean is most concentrated near land. You can't remove the organic solvents, pesticides, fertilizer residues, petroleum seepages, and all the other garbage with which we've littered the seas.

Saltwater Mixes

The seawater mixes available today are the result of an enormous amount of research by marine scientists, who have formulated various mixes for the optimum health, growth, and survivability of the captive organisms we keep in our aquaria. Although the water you just scoop out of the ocean is natural, it is also of unknown composition. So, what's wrong with that? Plenty!

Ocean water is not sterile; it is teeming with life. Even a bucketful of what seems to be just water is full of bacteria, and a myriad of minute plants and animals (plankton). Almost all of those living things in the seemingly empty bucket of sea water are not going to survive in the closed system of your aquarium. A few are actually going to bloom frantically in the absence of natural controls, but very shortly they're all going to die, and their decomposition will put a fatal overload on your bio-filter (which, if you're just setting up the tank, won't even be functioning yet). Getting natural sea water ready for use in an aquarium is an involved task, either of storage and decanting or of chlorinating and de-chlorinating. When you consider the pollutants, uncertain composition, and bio-load of natural sea water, you have the three strikes necessary to call it out. Play it safe and use an artificial salt mix.

Okay, so now that you are going to use premixed salt solutions, which one is best for your needs? Your dealer can assist you in that choice. All of the leading brands are fine to use, and at this point, as a beginner, you shouldn't be concerned about the small differences among them. By listening to your supplier's advice, you will get a brand that is stocked by the store, a brand that your dealer knows

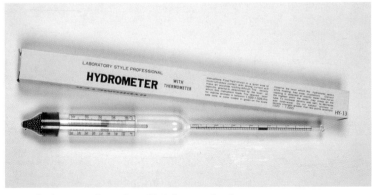

Some hydrometers have the added feature of a thermometer.

to be a quality product, and quite likely, the brand the fishes you'll be buying there are already used to.

Understanding Salinity/Specific Gravity

The salinity of water is measured by either parts per million (ppm) or specific gravity, which is a measure of the density of the water as compared to pure H_2O, which has specific gravity of 1.000. Oil is less dense, a hunk of lead is denser, and salt water is denser than fresh water.

You probably couldn't detect the slight weight difference between a bucket of fresh water and a bucket of salt water. The difference is vital to your fish, however, and it marks the physiological differences between marine organisms and other aquatic life.

Body fluids have a higher specific gravity than fresh water but a lower specific gravity than sea water. This means that freshwater fishes are faced with an osmotic problem of always taking on water into their cells, since water flows across membranes from an area of lower concentration (the lake) to the area of higher concentration (the cells of the fish's body). They need to excrete excess water and hang onto their body salts. Marine fishes have the opposite osmotic situation—they are always losing water from their tissues into the sea around them.

Salt Mixes

Good salt mixes are buffered, so hardness and pH are rarely a problem at first. The tank's pH, however, can drop dramatically when the tank is overstocked, the fish are overfed, or the filtration systems are over-relied on. As the pH falls because of the presence of acidic by-products of decomposition, the oxygen level also drops. You should therefore check the pH daily, at least until your bio-filter is established and you are used to the maintenance of your tank.

These fishes have to take in water all the time, excreting excess salts, and they are in constant danger of dehydrating their body tissues. The habits, kidneys, and gills of fishes all reflect this situation, and the understanding of this difference only makes one wonder how brackish water species, many of which will do well in both fresh and full salt water, as well as in various mixtures of the two, manage to survive!

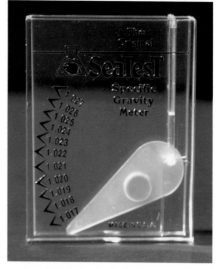

Plastic hydrometers with a swing arm are the most common type used by hobbyists. Be sure to rinse them with fresh water before and after each use.

Thus, a reliable hydrometer to measure the specific gravity is an absolute necessity, since it is the specific gravity of your aquarium water with which you are concerned, not the precise amount of salt to add. You will want to make a mix that reads between 1.020 and 1.025 at aquarium temperatures.

The Water Itself

Now that we've discussed the salt and how much to use, what about the water? If you use tap water for your freshwater tanks, it might seem appropriate to do the same for your marine tank, but it is not advisable. Since most tap water comes with a host of chemicals (mostly minerals) already dissolved in it, when you use it as a basis for artificial sea water you wind up, in effect, adding all those minerals to the carefully researched and formulated makeup of the mix. Having paid good money to get a properly balanced salt mix, you will throw it off balance with the tap water. Reverse osmosis (R.O.) water or distilled water is much better for your purposes, because

Outfitting Your Saltwater Aquarium

they are virtually devoid of any dissolved substances. Such pure water, when mixed with the salt mix, yields exactly the composition sea water that the scientists who formulated the mix intended, and which your fishes need to thrive in your care.

Once again, what looks like a complication—using water other than tap water—turns out to be the simpler choice, and it is free from the worries the simpler-looking choice entails.

Vacuuming

Vacuuming the substrate is important. This should be done regularly, even daily. While a thorough job is ideally coupled with a regular water change, smaller interim cleanings can consist of siphoning debris out of the gravel and straining the water through some filter medium and then returning it to the tank. You can also use one of the power filters that have gravel-vacuuming attachments, but again, remember to change the medium afterward—otherwise, you have done only a cosmetic cleaning. Any water loss from siphoning must, of course, be made up with salt water, but daily topping off of the tank's loss from evaporation should be with distilled or R.O. water, as the salt is left behind when the water evaporates.

Vacuuming your aquarium's gravel is a chore that should be done as frequently as possible.

Equipment

Keep in mind that your goal, at least at first, is to make as stable an environment as you can for your fishes while still keeping things simple; there will be time to fine-tune your marine husbandry later. The first area that you'll want to explore is that of filtration.

Marine aquariums that have more than just fish in them will need good, strong filtration.

Important Aspects of Filtration

There is nothing wrong with saltwater setups that have as much or more room devoted to the filtration system as they do to the aquarium itself, but your first attempt at saltwater fishes doesn't have to be that complicated. Likewise, you should not let current debates regarding aquarium setup deter you from starting in the hobby. Yes to sand or no to sand? Yes to an undergravel filter (UGF) or no to a UGF? Yes this or no that? The reason these debates exist is that there are no concrete rules about marine aquaria, and for every attempt someone makes to issue one, there is at least one experienced hobbyist who disproves the "rule" by the successful practice of its opposite.

Let's start with the pieces of equipment you're already familiar with. Circulation and aeration are, of course, also concerns of the marine aquarist. In fact, because salt water cannot hold as much dissolved oxygen as fresh water at the same temperature, aeration is even more important in the marine tank. Air pumps, power filters, and powerheads are all useful for this purpose, just as they are for freshwater tanks.

Likewise, the three types of filtration that you are probably familiar with already have their place in the saltwater system. The use of mechanical filtration media such as polyester fibers, gravel, or woven filter pads traps suspended particles and keeps the water looking clean. Outside power filters or canister filters are widely used to provide this type of filtration in saltwater tanks. Remember, though, that until you clean the filter medium, the garbage is still exposed to the tank's water, even if it is located outside the actual aquarium, and it continues to feed bacteria or to leach substances into the water the same as if it were still in the tank. Clean the filters often, and as always, remember that frequent water changes and siphoning of the substrate are major contributions to water quality.

Using Activated Carbon

You are undoubtedly familiar with using carbon as a type of chemical filtration. Many marine aquarists use other chemical filtration media in addition to activated carbon, and they tend to use more expensive, higher grade carbon as compared to their freshwater peers. The sensitivity of marine organisms to chemical pollutants in their water makes it doubly important to keep the water as free from invisible dissolved contaminants as from cloudiness and sediment. The desire to prevent algal blooms motivates the use of the higher grades of carbon, which are more efficient and are free of phosphates, as well as the various resins that remove selected contaminants. For your first marine tank, you can rely on quality carbon and regular water changes to maintain water quality.

Canister filters are the common location for chemical media in saltwater tanks, but regular power filters can also be used. Because of the initial dangers of pollutant buildup in newly established tanks, it is wise to fill filters exclusively with carbon at first. When the carbon is due for replacement (follow your dealer's and the manufacturer's recommendations), you can refill the canister with a variety of media if you wish.

Undergravel Filters (UGFs)

Now considered to be "old technology," UGFs have played an important role in the success of many marine hobbyists through the years. UGFs are basic in design, consisting of a large, perforated plastic plate that sits about 1-inch above the aquarium's bottom glass, and several lift tubes, through which water travels upward, pulling dirty water through the plate to be filtered. The space created by the suspended plate allows the growth of both aerobic and anaerobic bacteria to proliferate and convert toxic ammonia and nitrites to less toxic nitrates.

UGF's

A UGF permits the substrate in the tank to function as colonizing sites for the bacteria necessary to convert ammonia to nitrites and nitrites to nitrates, and it supplies them with the required constant supply of oxygenated water.

The aquarium's water is pulled through this plate by a series of lift tubes, which are powered by either air pumps or powerheads. The volume of water that is circulated through the UGF is directly dependant on the size and strength of the air pumps or powerheads used. Most UGFs have two to four lift tubes per UGF plate, depending on the size of the aquarium where the UGF is employed.

As with all filters, UGFs become clogged and need to be periodically cleaned. The best way to do this is by using a gravel vacuum while doing a water change. Because you should be performing partial water changes on a regular basis anyway, it's always best to spend some time cleaning a section of the aquarium's gravel. For example, if your aquarium is 3 feet long and you perform a 10-percent water change weekly, then a good idea would be to gravel vacuum a 1-foot section with each water change. This way, every three weeks you'll have gravel vacuumed your entire aquarium.

There are many tricks and techniques to utilizing a UGF to its maximum efficiency, and with some time, practice, and patience, you can use these "primitive" filters with quite impressive results.

Sump-style filters are commonly used in marine aquariums. This unit employs a filter bag as well as a protein skimmer for added filtration.

Wet-Dry Filters

Wet-dry filtration is based on the fact that air contains thousands of times more oxygen than does oxygen-saturated water. By placing a porous or fibrous medium under a spray or trickle of water, the filter provides not only suitable sites for bacterial colonization but also oxygen levels far superior to those obtainable in any submerged system. The "dry" filter medium is in fact wet, but just barely. Covered with only a film of water, the bacteria benefit from the extremely high oxygen concentration of the air while still remaining wet enough to survive. The surface area thus required for bio-filtration is considerably reduced from that needed by submerged filters, with a single bio-wheel providing the bio-filtration of about 30 pounds (14 kg) of gravel.

Such wet-dry filters have other advantages as well. Because the water splashing onto the medium is pre-filtered, there is very little maintenance needed. The medium does not have to be cleaned, which means the bacteria can continue to grow undisturbed.

Bio-Wheel Filters

A power filter with a bio-wheel is also a valuable addition or alternative to other filters used on a marine system. Either, or both, should provide efficient bio-filtration and aeration. Many other bio-filters, such as wet-dry and fluidized bed filters, are excellent devices, but they are neither as simple nor as inexpensive as most types of bio-wheel filters, which usually hang on the back of the aquarium.

Fluidized Bed Filters

The fluidized bed filter basically takes UGF filtration out of the aquarium, eliminating the disadvantages of such a system and optimizing the use of the surface

Hang-on bio-wheel filters are very popular and useful marine aquarium filters.

areas of the sand particles for bacterial colonization. Over the next few years, fluidized bed filters will undoubtedly undergo considerable improvements and expansion of features.

Lighting

You have probably noticed the large proportion of advertising devoted to marine lighting systems. You'll see multiple-bulb designs, such as HO and VHO bulbs and metal halide systems, and you will also see prices that will make you think the decimals have been accidentally moved to the right.

The biggest reason for the concern about lighting in marine tanks is that many saltwater invertebrates, most noticeably the coelenterates (e.g., corals and anemones), require high intensity, full spectrum lighting because of their symbiotic zooxanthellae, which live in their tissues

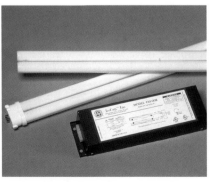

Power compact lighting is very efficient at illuminating a marine aquarium.

Outfitting Your Saltwater Aquarium

and photosynthesize. The same zooxanthellae are also responsible for the coloration that the corals reflect.

Since you should be starting with a fish-only tank, the only lighting necessary is what you need to properly enjoy the beauty of your fish. A regular aquarium fluorescent fixture will be fine. Complicated lighting systems are something that you can wait to tackle in the future.

Biological Filtration

The different types of biological filtration probably get more attention in the marine hobby than any other type of water-quality control. This is one of those areas in which you must not let the plethora of data, divergent scientific viewpoints, and conflicting advertising claims overwhelm you. You will hear about dozens of filters, special maintenance systems, computer-controlled monitoring systems, and wonder products that let you go years and years without changing water. This is not the forum to debate the pros and cons of all this technology. As you grow in the hobby, you will become familiar with the high-tech options open to you, and you will be able to discuss them with people who have tried them and allow you to make up your own mind.

Tests and Testing Equipment

You are used to making tests and measurements in your freshwater aquarium, and you will need to keep track of the chemistry of your marine tank as well. The hydrometer has already been mentioned as a required piece of equipment. The clear acrylic floating-needle type is quite popular and easy to use; just be sure you don't get any air bubbles in it, or they'll throw off your reading considerably.

Older style glass floating hydrometers that ride higher in the water as salinity increases are also quite serviceable. Whatever type of

Test kits are important to have and use. Be familiar with what you need to test for, and perform the tests as recommended by the manufacturer.

hydrometer you use, make sure that you read the scale correctly and follow the manufacturer's instructions. You want to maintain a specific gravity of 1.020 to 1.025.

Suitable Kits

A few test kits can be used in both fresh and salt water, but many cannot. Make sure the kits you use are suitable for saltwater testing. You will find a large variety of test kits for checking everything in your salt water, from pH to copper and iron concentrations, and from calcium ion concentration to O_2 saturation. So, which do you need?

You should obtain and use the saltwater equivalents of the hardness, pH, nitrite, and ammonia tests that you would use on a freshwater tank. A nitrate test kit is also a good idea, because it will let you know how effective your water changes are. For a fish-only tank, these tests should suffice. The total hardness and carbonate hardness should be high; keep the pH above 8.0, ammonia and nitrite levels as close to zero as possible, and nitrate levels below 30 ppm.

Thermometer

One other familiar and necessary device that needs no explanation

Outfitting Your Saltwater Aquarium

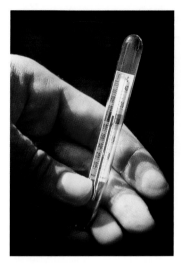

is the thermometer. Remember that one of the ways that the ocean is more stable than most bodies of fresh water is in its temperature, which does not experience the wide variation that streams, rivers, and ponds can undergo. The tank's temperature should be monitored constantly, so a reliable thermometer should be a permanent part of the setup.

A thermometer is an essential piece of equipment to own.

Temperature Control

Most marine tropical fishes are best kept at 75° to 80°F (23.8°-26.6° C), so a reliable heater is a necessity. The acceptable temperature range is narrow because of the stable nature of most marine environments. Influences such as change of seasons, rainy periods, flooding, and solar heating can drastically affect the temperature of bodies of fresh water. Marine organisms, except for a few specialized creatures such as estuary or tidal pool inhabitants, are not exposed to this type of variation. That is why the marine hobby is concerned with aquarium chillers as well as heaters.

Chillers are one solution to summertime temperatures, and they come in all sizes and capacities for different-size setups. Even the less expensive ones available for a modest marine setup needed to bring down the temperature only a few degrees is

Heaters are used to prevent an aquarium's water from falling below a certain temperature.

not cheap. Another alternative, however, is to air condition the room in which you have the aquarium, giving you, your family, and your fish the benefit of reduced summer temperatures.

Remember that salt water, which already has less dissolved oxygen than fresh, loses even more oxygen-carrying capacity as the temperature rises, so extra summertime aeration is extremely beneficial. Evaporation, which can be increased by both adding more aeration and by setting a fan to blow across the water surface, removes a lot of heat from an aquatic system. Just remember to keep the water level up and the specific gravity correct by replacing evaporation with distilled or R.O. water. Excess heat is a concern, but fishes are less susceptible than many invertebrates to overheating, so you do not have to be quite as concerned as a frantic reef hobbyist during a summer heat wave.

Protein Skimmers

You will not get far in the marine hobby without hearing about protein skimmers. They're simple, effective, and, by most people's standards, essential in any marine tank for the removal of organic pollutants before they get a chance to break down. Skimmers significantly decrease the load on the bio-filter, and consequently, they reduce the buildup of toxins in the tank. But if they're so good, why don't you use one in your freshwater aquarium?

The nature of salt water is such that air bubbles foam up more in it. You may have noticed that the airstones in marine tanks seem to put out a

Protein skimmers are excellent pieces of equipment that are used to remove insoluble wastes from the salt water.

much foggier stream of bubbles than those in freshwater tanks. If you watch the bubbles breaking the surface, you will see that saltwater bubbles are smaller and more long lived; vigorous aeration (including from waves) produces a "suds" you will not see in unpolluted fresh water. This fact underlies the technology of a protein skimmer, which is operated by either an air pump with a special airstone or by a venturi to introduce the air bubbles into the water stream.

The skimmer works because many substances, most notably organic compounds, adhere to the surface of bubbles. By forcing a stream of bubbles through a narrow column of water from the tank, many of these contaminants are flushed out as the foam created by the bubbles is skimmed off and trapped in a waste receptacle.

Skimmers come in many varieties; some fit inside the tank, some are external, and others fit into the sump of trickle filters. There are

even power filters that incorporate skimmers within themselves. You needn't get fancy—just select one that is rated for your size tank or slightly larger.

There are two major drawbacks to skimmers. The first, much more of a concern in invertebrate or reef tanks, is that skimmers can remove beneficial substances such as trace elements along with the contaminants they so effectively trap. Your regular water changes should offset this problem in your fish-only tank.

The protein skimmer that you use should directly correlate to the size of your aquarium—the larger the tank, the larger the skimmer.

Skimmers work only when they are properly adjusted, and you have to practice to get them adjusted correctly. They also need constant maintenance, such as daily emptying of the foam collection cup and rigorously regular replacement of the airstones. In this case, however, two arguments work toward the inclusion of protein skimmers—even in a hobbyist's first marine system.

There is no real alternative to protein skimmers. You can avoid the super-colossal filter that takes up the whole space under the tank and then some and still get a fair replacement in a bio-wheel power filter that hangs on the back of the tank. The protein skimmer, however, is extremely simple, even minimal, in design and has no close alternative other than a constant stream of new salt water flowing through the tank. While extremely simple and wonderfully efficient, the impracticality and expense of that solution make the skimmer much more attractive to a beginner's scheme.

A skimmer is not an absolute necessity; people used to keep marine fish without them, and some still do. The odds are much more in your favor, however, if you include this simple accessory. Admittedly, it requires precise adjustment and careful care, but it will make an enormous difference to your fishes and therefore also to you. Get one, read the instructions, ask your dealer for a demonstration and for hints, and then set it up. Make only minor adjustments, and then wait to see how things are going.

You should not panic and rush to readjust things if you find that your skimmer decreases its output over time. A newly set up system will have much more organic waste than a balanced system with an established bio-filter. Also, if you add a skimmer to a tank that has been stocked for some time, you will notice a great decrease after it removes the initial backlog of wastes.

Ultraviolet Sterilizers

Ultraviolet sterilizers (UV sterilizers) get much more attention by marine hobbyists than by freshwater fishkeepers. One reason for this is the need to eliminate microalgae in reef tanks. In addition, marine fishes are more susceptible to infections and diseases than freshwater species, at least more so than those freshwater fishes that have been bred in captivity for decades. These devices kill microorganisms, clearing up water and preventing disease by attacking the root causes—microscopic creatures.

The two types used are ozone generators and UV sterilizers. Both can be dangerous (to you and to your fishes), both are expensive, and both require technical knowledge to maintain them. While the ozone generator is basically a one-time purchase even though it needs considerable regular attention, the UV sterilizer, though fairly easy to keep operating, needs frequent (every six months maximum) replacement of the expensive UV bulb.

If the expense is not a problem, UV sterilizers, once installed in a filtration circuit, are simple enough to operate, and as long as you keep fresh lamps in them they provide a real benefit, both in keeping your fish healthy and in keeping the water clear. You should purchase a unit rated for a slightly larger tank than you'll be using, since the output of the UV bulb begins to drop off immediately, and a unit barely ample for your setup will quickly be working below minimum effectiveness. This is one of those pieces of equipment, however, that you can forgo in your first marine tank.

Substrate and Decorations

As a freshwater hobbyist, you may be thinking about a planted saltwater tank. Forget it. For the most part, marine plants are not like terrestrial or freshwater plants, which are predominantly higher (vascular) flowering plants. Seaweeds are macroalgae, their "leaves" basically long strings of simple cells similar to single-celled algae.

Macroalgae, especially species of the genus *Caulerpa*, are popular in reef tanks, but they have two major drawbacks for you. One, they are a tasty snack for almost any fish and will be grazed away

Make sure that all of the decorations placed in your saltwater aquarium are inert (unreactive).

in no time, and two, they are definitely not easy to keep. Like those invertebrates that incorporate photosynthesizing organisms in their tissues, macroalgae need intense light; they promptly die and foul the tank when they don't get it. If you like the looks of the seaweed you see in your dealer's or a friend's tank, start saving both money and knowledge for your first mini-reef tank, complete with live rock, live sand, and live plants. For now, stick with inanimate decorations.

Almost none of the inanimate items you decorate your freshwater tank with are suitable for your marine aquarium, however, as they are either totally inappropriate or inferior to something else. The major exceptions to this are ceramic or plastic ornaments and plastic plants. Many hobbyists consider these unnatural in freshwater tanks and even less aesthetically suited to saltwater ones, but they are not hazardous. If you like them, use them. Your fishes will avail themselves of the hiding places they provide without worrying about whether they're natural enough.

Driftwood, the natural decorative water conditioner for soft, acid, "black water" tanks, is a definite no-no. The tannins it leaches into the water are alien to any marine environment except brackish man-

Live rock is an excellent decoration for nearly all saltwater aquarium applications.

grove swamps, and their tendency to soften and acidify water is at cross purposes with your highly buffered, hard, alkaline saltwater mix.

When acquiring rocks for your freshwater tank, you were cautioned no doubt about various types suitable only for salt water, such as limestone and coral rock. Now, most of the freshwater-safe rocks you are familiar with can be used in saltwater tanks, but being largely from terrestrial locales (streams, waterfalls, river gorges), they do not look anywhere near as natural in the marine tank. In addition, the soluble minerals in saltwater-only rocks help to buffer your water against a fatal pH drop.

The same is true for coral or dolomite substrate. Besides looking more like an ocean bottom than quartz gravel, coral sand or crushed dolomite serves to keep hardness and pH at optimum levels in a marine tank. Sand is also the preferred substrate for those fish species that burrow into it and can be inhibited or even injured by coarser gravel.

Coral—that is, the dead, bleached skeletons of colonial hard corals—used to be the traditional decoration for marine tanks. Recently, the loss of reef ecosystems has focused concern on any harvesting of marine species, and fortunately for the hobbyist, plastic replicas of many coralline structures are now available. These artificial corals are very convincing, are a snap to keep clean, and usually cost less than the natural models.

You will want to fashion rocks and corals with epoxy or sealant into structures that provide sufficient hiding places to make your pets feel secure enough to act naturally and to provide them refuge from aggression. Other than that, your taste and your budget should be your only guides.

Cycling the Tank

You're all set up. The water is in and at the proper salinity, the filters are running, the lights are on, the skimmer is bubbling away, and the heater is maintaining the proper temperature. Ready to stock it with fishes? No!

The nitrogen cycle must first be started so that the bio-filter can begin to grow. Over the years, there have been various proposals for how to do this, from adding one fish at a time over a period of a couple of months to feeding the empty tank as if it had fishes in it, from seeding the tank with ammonium chloride to many others, some more bizarre than promising.

In addition, there are bacterial cultures on the market, specifically made for saltwater systems, which give the bio-filter a jump-start by supplying a concentration of the appropriate species of nitrifying bacteria. Claims as grand as "add culture, water, and fish" abound, but although these products can vastly shorten cycling times, you should not rely on them to make the tank instantly ready for a full complement of fishes.

Live sand can be used to help cycle a new marine aquarium and is available from most aquarium supply shops.

How should you cycle the new marine tank? Remember that caution can make up for a whole lot of technology. To be safe, add a proprietary culture of one or two fish, and feed them sparingly for a couple of weeks, and monitor the water's quality. After that time, if the water still tests within acceptable limits, add another fish or two, but keep a close eye on the ammonia, nitrite, and nitrate levels. They should peak and decline in that order over a period of up to six weeks. At that point you can stock the tank to its capacity.

Another alternative is to borrow a bio-filter. You can do this by using gravel from an established marine tank that uses a UGF as a substantial portion of the substrate in your new tank. You can also place several sponge filters in an established marine tank for a month before you set up your tank, and then put them in—instant bio-filter. Or, if you are using a bio-wheel filter, you can take the bio-wheels from an established marine tank and use them on the filter on your new tank. The first and last of these alternatives have the drawback of depriving the old tank of much of its bio-filter, but it can work, especially if your new tank is smaller than your friend's established tank, which would let you leave some of the old filter media behind.

Fishes & Invertebrates

The fishes you choose for your tank will, of course, be dependent on your budget, your preferences, and what is available where you live at the time you wish to set up your aquarium. There are, however, quite a few that you should not purchase, either because they are not hardy enough for a beginner or because they are not suited to aquarium life no matter how skilled the aquarist is.

A sampling of beginners' fishes is just that, a sampling. Your future favorite might not be listed here, and you may despise one that is listed. You will not find Moorish idols here or any other high-priced, hard-to-keep species. Tangs are omitted, despite their frequent appearance in dealers' tanks, because they fare better in the tanks of more experienced hobbyists. Butterflyfishes and angelfishes, though gorgeous, are not listed, because you should wait a little while before taking on these more difficult species. Sharks, rays, moray eels, and other titillating denizens of the deep are conspicuously absent also, as these species are for a public aquarium or the tanks of an advanced marine aquarist. Even the snowflake moray, an otherwise easy-to-keep species, is going to present feeding and escape headaches you don't need the first time around.

Taken as a general guide, the suggestions here will get you pointed in the right direction, but the rules for husbandry already discussed in this book will serve you well for almost any fish you knowledgeably select from a reliable dealer's tank.

Damselfishes

Damselfishes are the guppies of the saltwater hobby in the sense that they are the first fish for many aquarists—easy to keep, colorful, and interesting—and many species have even been bred in captivity. People who start with damsels often continue in the hobby. In fact, like experienced and jaded freshwater hobbyists who "rediscover" guppies, many marine aquarists buy a group of hardy damsels to

There are many types of damsels for hobbyists to choose from. An orange-tailed blue devil is pictured here.

Green chromis usually do well in aquariums as long as they are purchased as a small school of four or more.

cycle a new tank, but by the time the bio-filter is operating, they've become enamored of them and don't want to part with them.

Damsels are custom-made beginner fishes. They come in a wide variety of colors and patterns, from black and white, either spots or stripes, to brilliant solid colors, including several bright blue species commonly called "blue devils." They are relatively undemanding, hardy, and eager feeders—something that cannot be said for many other marine species. Just about the only drawback is their territoriality, a problem with most species of damselfishes.

Some hobbyists recommend having just one individual of several species of damsels, because intra-specific aggression is usually the worst. By choosing dissimilar-looking species, you can avoid a lot of the territorial battling. Another technique, also used by African rift lake cichlid hobbyists, is to keep several of a given species, which actually diminishes the aggression by diffusing each agonistic act among many targets. Often a fish is so busy watching over its shoulder for the next attack that it doesn't launch one of its own.

By starting with a group of small fish and providing plenty of cover and room for territories, you should be successful in achieving a

Fishes & Invertebrates

suitable if tense harmony. Adding a new fish to a tank full of damsels is, however, like adding a match to a keg of dynamite. If you must do it, take out all the decorations, mix them up to dissolve territory boundary markers, and preferably place more than one newcomer at a time.

Anemonefishes

Anemonefishes, which include the stereotypical marine aquarium fish, the clownfish, are specialized damselfishes that have adapted to life within the nematocyst-armed tentacles of the deadly (to most other fishes) sea anemones. Not only are clownfish hardy, fairly easy to breed, and fascinatingly colorful, they also are always a hit as they nestle among the stinging anemone's waving limbs. And while they normally spawn in or near their host anemone, clownfishes are even bred commercially like cichlids—one pair per bare tank, with a flat spawning surface. Captive-bred clownfishes are available and worth the higher price they may carry.

The communalism between the clownfish and its host anemone is one of the better-known wonders of the coral reef, familiar even to some people who know nothing else about marine life. The temp-

These tomato clowns are enjoying the presence of an anemone, which is not needed in their aquarium but certainly welcomed.

A Note About Anemones

Anemones are not for beginners, no matter how hard you try. They are among those invertebrates that need all that fancy expensive lighting, and they are particularly fussy about water conditions. They are hard to feed properly. For a beginner, they are trouble just waiting to happen. They also smell incredibly bad when they die and start turning into a slimy goo in your tank.

tation to get a pair of clowns and a colorful anemone will be great, but you must resist buying an anemone.

Angelfishes

Between size constraints and feeding problems, most angelfishes and butterflyfishes would be excluded from a beginner's marine tank, even if they weren't quarrelsome and scrappy. Unfortunately, the husbandry problems associated with many of these species are equally matched by their outrageously gorgeous coloration. All is not lost, however, because there are many beautiful and peaceful pygmy angels of the genus *Centropyge* that are possible candidates for your first marine tank.

Coral beauty angels are very colorful and long lived in most aquariums of 30 gallons (114 l) or more.

All of these species are grazers, some being totally herbivorous, but algae and green foods are a lot easier to supply than the living sponges many larger angels require. Most of the pygmy angels will also accept meaty foods. Though not as hardy as some of the larger species, and perhaps better saved for later on in your first tank, after you have a bit of experience, these fishes are nevertheless relatively undemanding. They are a nice step up in challenge from the "cast iron" damselfishes.

Groupers

You are probably familiar with the giant groupers that greet similar-sized scuba divers. There are a few species from the grouper and sea bass family that are small enough for large aquaria, such as the six-line grouper, which has many (actually more than six) white lines on its dark body that turn to rows of dotted lines as the fish matures.

Baby panther groupers are commonly offered for sale, and they are irresistibly patterned, with terrific personalities. Their adult size of 2 to 3 feet (60-90 cm), however, should give you pause as you gaze longingly into your dealer's tank.

More suitable are the dwarf relatives of the groupers, the fairy basslets, grammas, and dottybacks. Two stunning species are the strawberry Pseudochromis and the royal gramma, both of which are magenta in front and orange yellow in back. They are hardy and beautiful but often extremely quarrelsome and territorial. They cannot be kept with their own kind or species of similar habits, though one of them in a mixed-species tank is a real showstopper.

Other Good Things in Small Packages

There are other tiny gems suitable for your new marine aquarium. These include the hawkfishes, which perch on a piece of coral or rock like a bird of prey waiting to swoop down on its dinner as it swims below.

Long-nosed hawkfishes are interesting fish to observe in marine aquariums as they bounce from rock to rock in search of food.

Various gobies, including the neon goby, have the distinction of being small, hardy, extremely colorful, and peaceful. A bright display can be set up with a variety of small gobies. Similarly, many of the smaller wrasses, such as the cleaner wrasse and the reindeer wrasse are peaceful additions to the community setting.

Blennies

The diminutive blennies deserve separate mention, because they have unique assets and liabilities. They are extremely hardy, and like most other bottom-dwelling fishes with reduced swim bladders, comically interesting. They are also some of those "personality" fishes that endear themselves to their owners with such things as eating out of their hands. While some species are quite colorful, many don't match the neon elegance of other marine tropicals.

Night Life

Several largely nocturnal species, with the concomitant extra-large eyes, are hardy and suitable for the beginner's marine tank. Most notable among them are the cardinalfishes, which are timid and need to have sedate tankmates, and the squirrelfishes, which are boisterous and active (though not so much through the day) and are poor companions for retiring species such as the cardinalfishes.

There are many types of fishes that become active during darkness. This cardinal fish is just one of them.

If acclimated gradually to a brighter and brighter tank, provided with plenty of daytime hiding spots and caves, and if they are fed during the day, these interesting, mostly red fishes will adjust to a less nocturnal lifestyle.

Cowfishes and Boxfishes

Cowfishes and boxfishes are related to puffers and porcupinefishes. These unlikely-looking creatures are peaceful and interesting aquarium residents, but when disturbed, they produce a toxic substance that can poison any of the tank inhabitants, including themselves! Transporting these fishes is therefore a tricky business, though once established in a tank, they are not too easily provoked. Although their main appeal is their unusual appearance, they are generally hardy and easy-to-keep pets.

Toxic Turkeys

Turkeyfishes, more commonly called lionfishes or scorpion fishes, are beautiful marine tropicals. However, they can be dangerous to the hobbyist who is unaware of their venomous spines. This venom is toxic enough that you should not attempt to see how resistant you are to it. The fishes themselves, however, make good aquarium inhabitants, and they are even appropriate for a community tank in which none of the other residents is small enough to be swallowed. Live fishes are the lionfishes' preferred fare.

Like many other venomous creatures, lionfishes are strikingly colored. Again, like many other venomous creatures, they

Lionfishes, also called turkeyfishes, are popular with hobbyists who are looking for a marine predator.

are placid and easygoing, able to be kept in mixed or single-species groups.

Obviously, you should be extremely careful when moving a lionfish or when maintaining an aquarium containing one. No matter how tame it is, do not stick your hand into the tank without placing some sort of partition (a rectangle of plastic "egg crate" light diffuser works well) between it and the area you need to service. And of course, the tank needs to be positioned and covered in such a way that children cannot gain access to it. In general, toxic pets of any type are not recommended for households with children who have not yet reached adolescence.

Toxic Uglies

Hobbyists sometimes keep some other poisonous and/or grotesque species. The stonefishes, toadfishes, and anglerfishes (frogfishes) are hardy although "cosmetically challenged." They make unusually hardy and interesting pets, but all of them have *big* mouths, and

Stonefishes, toadfishes, and anglerfishes all make interesting and unusual residents in a marine aquarium.

Fishes & Invertebrates

some of them are able to engulf fishes almost the same size as they are; they can quickly turn a community tank into a single-fish tank. And beware of the venomous spines on the stonefishes and toadfishes!

Mandarins

Mandarins are best left for experienced hobbyists because they can be difficult to feed properly.

As tiny, beautiful, and inoffensive as the stonefishes are big, ugly, and dangerous, mandarins are hardy, very colorful, and comical fishes. They usually do not get along well with their own kind and therefore should be kept singly or as a pair if you can get an established pair. They are bottom hugging and fairly inactive, and they require non-boisterous tankmates. These traits make them one of the few species you might be able to keep with seahorses.

Jawfishes

Jawfishes are fun and active fishes that do well in most stable marine tanks.

Many of these unusual fishes are seen normally only from the gills up, as they keep the rest of their body in their home burrows in the sand. At any sign of danger, they retreat backward into their holes. They are peaceful with other fishes and with others of their own species as long as there is sufficient room for each to have its own burrow. As with most nervous, timid fishes, the jawfishes' tankmates must be chosen with care to avoid their being intimidated or harassed.

Invertebrates

You will find various marine invertebrates that are actually suitable for your first tank offered for sale through your local aquarium supply shop. Some crustaceans (crabs, lobsters, and shrimp), for example, are hardy, colorful, interesting, and inexpensive. While many of them will prey on other invertebrates, most get along well with fishes large enough to avoid capture. In addition, they are excellent litter patrols, picking up any food particles the other tank inhabitants miss. A perennial favorite is the hermit crab, cousin of the popular terrestrial species.

Mollusks are generally a poor choice for your aquarium for a variety of reasons. Many of them are specialized feeders. With some it is difficult to tell if they are alive or not, and they can pollute a tank fast if their demise goes unnoticed. The squids and octopuses are predatory escape artists, who if provoked, can poison everything in the tank, including themselves, with their defensive ink emissions. Some of them can even give you a nasty venomous bite. The octopuses are also highly intelligent and dexterous, able to learn to uncork bottles and open hatches to get food. Think what their eight flexible and muscular arms can do to your filter, heater, hood, etc.

Skunk cleaner shrimp are very attractive and do a great job of picking small parasites from your fishes.

Snails are often used in both freshwater and marine aquariums to reduce the growth of nuisance algae.

Certain snails can be useful in keeping down unwanted algal growth, and they and their shell-less cousins, the nudibranchs, can be flamboyantly colorful. Some of those beautiful nudibranchs, however, are very predatory, with a few of them specialized to feed on other nudibranchs, and some cone snails are so venomous that they have been featured as the murder weapon in baffling whodunits.

It is best to restrict your first invertebrates to a small crab or shrimp or two. Cleaner shrimps, which are highly colored to advertise their don't-eat-me role as parasite pickers, may even indulge in that behavior if you house them with compatible fishes. A good rule of thumb is to assume your crustaceans are extremely territorial and to limit them to one of a species per tank, even though a few of them get along well communally. Almost all of them are cave or burrow dwellers, so plenty of nooks and crannies are important, especially so that they can hide safely after molting, before their new exoskeleton hardens.

There are several species of shrimps that form symbiotic relationships with certain hardy goby/blenny species. The excavating shrimp houses and scavenges after the goby, who serves as an early warning against predators; the shrimp feeds off the table scraps of its host/guest. Such a pair makes for some fascinating inhabitants of a marine tank, as long as you get compatible species.

Foods &
Feeding

Feeding marine fishes is not much different from feeding freshwater fishes. Very small but frequent feedings using a wide variety of high-quality foods will provide your pets with the nutrition they need while preventing problems resulting from the decomposition of uneaten foods.

Foods

The main problem comes in actually getting the fishes to eat. That is something that freshwater hobbyists do not usually have to deal with very often. There are many commercial flake and pellet foods formulated for the specific dietary needs of marine fishes, but many species need the coaxing of frozen, if not living, food organisms. While freshwater organisms can be useful in feeding marine tropicals, they must be balanced with marine foods, because certain fatty acids are missing in freshwater species. A steady diet of feeder goldfish, for example, will leave you with a malnourished lionfish, while various species of marine baitfish or pieces of a saltwater fish offer a much better alternative.

Vegetable Matter

Leafy greens make excellent additions to the diet of most marine fishes.

Many marine fishes need vegetable matter in their diet, and you can supplement the algae that will naturally grow in your tank with blanched fresh vegetables such as zucchini, spinach, or peas. There are also excellent commercial preparations for herbivorous species, many based on the highly nutritious *Spirulina* algae.

Living Foods

Live foods should also be utilized in the diet of marine fishes on a regular basis. Brine shrimp can be purchased live or frozen. In most cases, however, true marine food animals are too rare to use them all the time. Large fishes also take earthworms, preferably offered to them individually. With all the other freshwater food animals, precise dispensing is the best way to avoid problems.

It is important to be aware of the survival times of the indi-

Earthworms are more commonly used as food for freshwater fishes, but don't underestimate their value for marine species, too.

Live brine shrimp are very popular with marine hobbyists, but don't feed them alone; they need to be supplemented with a more balanced food.

vidual food organisms in salt water. Tubifex die particularly quickly, within a few minutes. White worms and cyclops survive two to three hours. Daphnia are usually already dead within ten minutes. Midge larvae can live for up to 24 hours in salt water and thus remain attractive to the fishes. A temperature shock shortens the survival times or even leads to the immediate death of live foods.

Frozen Foods

The remains of frozen foods must be removed from the tank quickly, namely within a few hours. Shellfish, crab, shrimp, squid, and fish fillet are all good candidates and can be further supplemented with offerings of fish eggs (roe), ant pupae, lean beef heart, and mealworms.

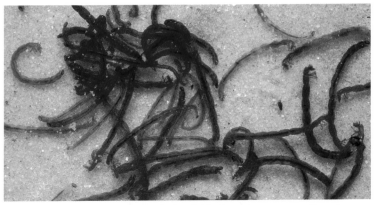

Frozen bloodworms are commonly available from the majority of pet shops and serve as an excellent food for most marine fishes.

Helpful Hints to Feeding Frozen Foods

Feeding frozen foods is highly recommended due to their diversity and freshness. Most frozen foods are easily broken into smaller pieces and can therefore be stored and thawed in individual packages so as to not expose the whole lot to air on a daily basis. They have to be fed in a way that is safe for your fishes.

To feed a piece of frozen food to your fish, simply place the piece to be fed in a small volume of water taken directly from the aquarium. Next, allow the food to thaw completely, stirring gently so as not to break up the food too much. Thawing usually takes 15 minutes or so. Then, gently strain all of the water out of the thawing container by pouring the contents of the container through an appropriately sized net or by actually removing the food by hand. In the case of larger foods like whole fish or shrimp, rinse the foods in clean tank water before offering them. Formulations should be added slowly to prevent overfeeding, as should smaller foods like mysid shrimp and brine shrimp. Only feed as much as your fish will actively consume and not let hit the bottom of the aquarium. Feed frozen foods often, but when possible, alternate them with a high-quality prepared food.

Feeding

Generally, fishes should be fed daily. However, such a generalization is marked with controversy right from the start and needs to be made more specific. So what if we said that community fishes need to be fed daily, but predatory fishes need to be fed three times weekly? This is a little better, but what if we have a community of predatory fishes?

To further complicate matters, what about opportunistic predatory fishes or fishes that would not consume another animal unless it was there for the taking? Are marine angelfishes predatory? Not in the

Overfeeding

general sense, but they do prey on sponges. What we are getting at here is that all fish are basically predatory in one sense or another. This is an important concept to learn and understand. The feeding of fishes has more to do with opportunity and metabolism than anything else.

The fish's opportunity to eat depends largely on you, the hobbyist, and when you are going to offer it food. More often than not, they will eat—or try to eat—whatever you put in front of them. This can be good and bad. It is especially bad when you make a conscious

Large marine angelfishes need marine sponges in their diet.

Don't be afraid to experiment with different foods and a varied diet has many fringe benefits, such as better color, more vigor, and makes for a healthier fish overall.

decision to feed them the wrong foods and less of it than their body is telling them they need. It can be good when you make a similar decision and offer them the right foods in the right amounts at the right times.

Experimentation

Experimentation is important with our marine charges. Among the coral fishes, there appears to be a particularly pronounced tendency toward individual "tasters," while predatory fish eaters of the sea receive their ration only twice a week. All other species, for the most part, eat a varied diet. Most species can therefore be fed three to five times a week in small portions with little or no problems.

Diseases & Disorders

The old adage is right: A pound of cure is the cost of forgetting your ounce of prevention. In addition, when we're talking about marine fishes, that pound of cure is quite likely to be ineffective, and then the lives of your aquarium's inhabitants can be the cost. So make positive, proactive health practices part of your daily fish maintenance program, and you will prevent most problems from arising.

We've already covered many of these practices—water changes, proper filtration, stocking rates, and proper feeding. Also important is intense observation of your fishes, something you undoubtedly will be doing anyway, but be alert to subtle changes

When purchasing fishes, check for clear eyes and full fins, and make sure that they're eating well before you purchase them.

in appearance and behavior that can signal illness. Healthy fishes are hungry fishes, and any fish that refuses to eat needs careful watching. This brings up the importance of carefully selecting your fishes in the first place.

Selecting a Healthy Fish

As with freshwater fishes, you should inspect any potential purchases, plus the other fishes in the tank with them, for signs of illness or injury. Everything you are used to looking for in freshwater specimens applies here: Avoid white spots, red spots, bruises, open sores, heavy breathing, cottony growths, listlessness, and erratic swimming. These last two need a qualification. Marine fishes have evolved a wide variety of swimming patterns. The hopping of a goby, the hovering of a cowfish, or the dorsal fin ruddering of a seahorse are all unusual for other fishes, but not for them! And many marine tropicals normally have their fins unextended, so be careful not to diagnose normal fin postures as "clamped fins." As always, your reputable dealer can help explain what is normal for the species you are considering.

In addition, since refusal to eat is a common problem in wild-caught marine tropicals, you should only purchase fishes that you have seen eating. Ask the dealer to feed the fish, and don't accept any excuses for why they aren't eating. If they won't take food, don't take them home. Leave the overcoming of hunger strikes to experienced hobbyists, most of whom won't undertake the task anyway.

Your selection of fishes will be critical to the success of your aquarium, but you should not expect to make all the right decisions at first. After some time, you will learn which fishes you like and which you don't like, and you will become familiar with the disposition of each species. It is inevitable that you will want to purchase more of the fishes you like and get rid of those you do not like.

Quarantine

Once you get your new pet home, do not put it into your community tank. Put it into a quarantine tank. The quarantine tank can be small, say 10 gallons, and can be minimally decorated. Maybe just a hunk of PVC pipe or a clay pot can be used for a hiding "cave." A bare bottom is useful for keeping it clean.

Some fishes, like these banner fish, should be quarantined for at least a few weeks before being introduced to the main tank.

For filtration, if you are only going to set it up on occasion when you buy fish, you can use a seasoned sponge filter, which you keep running in the corner of your main tank the rest of the time to keep the bacterial culture alive.

Keep your new fish in here for a month or longer until you are certain it is free of parasites and disease and until it has recovered from the shocks and traumas of being netted, shipped, and reshipped. This not only keeps the newcomer from infecting your healthy tank but also gets it into the best condition before it has to face its new, already established tankmates.

New Fish Introductions

The introduction of new fishes is probably the most common way that problems are brought to an already established tank. Frequently, a fish will be sick, but there will be no outward manifestations of the problem. It will only gradually become apparent over a period of several days or weeks.

Identifying the Problem

It is inevitable that no matter how good a job you do of selecting healthy fish, setting up a quarantine tank for new fish, and maintaining your aquarium, at some point you will have a problem with sick or diseased fishes. This is not to be looked upon as a failure but merely the fact that most living things deteriorate as they grow older, and older organisms tend to have more problems. If you are maintaining your water quality by frequent partial water changes and monitoring your pH, you should be able to circumvent problems for a considerable length of time.

One of the ways that diseases can be brought into the aquarium is if you recently added new plants. All new additions to the tank

should be thoroughly disinfected with a strong solution of potassium permanganate before they are placed in the aquarium.

Something you might have to consider when determining what has caused a particular problem in your aquarium is the age of the fishes. Most livebearers live only two to three years, so if you have purchased mature fish initially, it is likely that they may be reaching the end of the line. This can be determined by several signs of old age, such as weight loss, subdued colors, humpbacks, and abnormal swimming motions. At this point, it might be best to remove a sick fish before it dies in the tank and causes additional problems in the community aquarium.

Basically, there are two types of problems that you will have to deal with when it comes to fish diseases. These are parasitic infestations and bacterial or fungal infections.

Parasitic Infestations
Many fish parasites are visible on the body of the fish after they reach a certain stage of development or have multiplied to a sufficient extent. Once you have detected these visible spots, it is up to

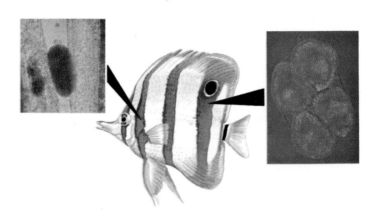

This diagram demonstrates the common areas where parasites take hold on a fish.

Lymphocystis is a virus that gives an appearance similar to that of a fungus.

Choosing the Right Meds

Ask your pet shop dealer which medications are best for your particular situation. Another disease similar to Ick is "velvet," caused by the parasite *Oodinium*. This disease is a bit more difficult to cure, but it can be done if you are diligent. Again, ask your pet shop dealer what he uses.

you to determine what they are and treat them accordingly. The most common aquarium parasite is Ick. It manifests itself by forming numerous white spots on the body and fins of the fish. It is easily cured using readily available commercial remedies.

You will find that several of the treatments used to combat parasitic infestations, such as acriflavine, contain a dye that will discolor your water. This dye allows the hobbyist to know that the medication is present. When you are using medications, it is important that you discontinue the use of activated carbon filtration so that the medication is not absorbed by the carbon and thereby rendered ineffective. It will still be important to maintain filtration, however, so remove the carbon from your filter and put the floss back in. (You may need to add gravel or marbles to an inside filter to hold it down.) Once you notice that the spots have disappeared for five days or more, you may consider the treatment completed, and it is then a good idea to change as much as 75 percent of the water, although a 50-percent water change is probably better.

Bacterial & Fungal Infections

Bacterial infections often become complicated by fungus. Basically, when the tank environment deteriorates to the extent that a bloom of bacteria has occurred, the bacteria attack weak fish that have open wounds and kill selected areas of flesh. Fungus soon grows on this dead flesh. If you notice small white tufts of hair-like filamentous material on your fishes, they have a fungal infection.

Read for Information

There are many excellent books on fish diseases. It is important that you get a copy as a reference guide so you can identify the problem and its solution as soon as possible. Offering first aid to your fishes will save you more than the value of a fish disease book. It is more efficient to identify an exact problem and treat it accordingly than to have to constantly replace dead fish or the entire community.

There are many drugs available at your pet shop that will cure fungal infections. Be careful when using some drugs (including dyes); the packages will carry information as to whether they are safe for all types of fishes. In some cases, certain drugs may kill your plants. It is always recommended that if only one or two fishes in a community aquarium are infected, these should be removed immediately to a small treatment or hospital tank, so the drug will not have to be used in the main tank. This will save money because you will be using less medication, and it will go a long way toward ensuring that other fishes are not exposed to the same disease.

Medications

When, despite your best precautions, your fish do fall ill to white spot (the saltwater "ick" caused by the protozoan *Cryptocaryon*) or some other malady, your dealer can help you in diagnosing and selecting treatment. The tried and true medication for saltwater fishes is copper, usually as copper sulfate. If you have invertebrates, remember that the lethal dose for them is about half the lethal dose for fishes, well within normal medication boundaries, and that for some inverts, any copper is deadly. There is also concern that copper will be taken up and stored in coral and sand, so a tank once treated with copper may never be able to be used for a reef tank without being totally cleaned and refitted with new materials.

Snails and other invertebrates don't react well to most medications. If you have to medicate your main tank, be sure that it is safe for invertebrates, too.

Most medications disturb or destroy the bacteria in your bio-filter as well, so treat a sick fish in a hospital tank if at all possible. That quarantine tank is perfect for this as well, but the bio-filter will need to be regrown afterward. With reasonable vigilance and consistent preventive care, your fish should thrive.

CONVERSION CHART

US UNITS	MULTIPLIED BY	EQUALS METRIC UNITS
Length		
Inches	2.5400	Centimeters
Feet	0.3048	Meters
Yards	0.9144	Meters
Miles	1.6093	Kilometers
Area		
Square inches	6.4516	Square centimeters
Square feet	0.0929	Square meters
Square yards	0.8361	Square meters
Acres	0.4047	Hectares
Volume		
Cubic feet	0.0283	Cubic meters
Cubic yards	0.7646	Cubic meters
Gallons	3.7854	Liters
Weight		
Foot-pounds	1.3830	Newton-meters
Pounds	0.4536	Kilograms

Temperature

Fahrenheit to Celsius: Subtract 32 from the Fahrenheit temperature. Divide the answer by 9, then multiply by 5.

Resources

MAGAZINES

Tropical Fish Hobbyist Magazine
1 T.F.H. Plaza
3rd & Union Avenues
Neptune City, NJ 07753
Phone: (732) 988-8400
E-mail: info@tfh.com
www.tfhmagazine.com

INTERNET RESOURCES

A World of Fish
www.aworldoffish.com

AquaLink
www.aqualink.com

Aquaria Central
www.aquariacentral.com

Aquarium Hobbyist
www.aquariumhobbyist.com

FINS: The Fish Information Service
http://fins.actwin.com

Fish Geeks
www.fishgeeks.com

Fish Index
www.fishindex.com

MyFishTank.Net
www.myfishtank.net

Reef Central
www.reefcentral.com

Reefs.Org
www.feef.org

Tropical Resources
www.tropicalresources.net

Water Wolves
http://forums.waterwolves.com

Wet Web Media
www.wetwebmedia.com

SOCIETIES & ORGANIZATIONS

Association of Aquarists
David Davis, Membership Secretary
2 Telephone Road
Portsmouth, Hants, England
PO4 0AY
Phone: 01705 798686

Canadian Association of Aquarium Clubs
Miecia Burden, Membership Coordinator
142 Stonehenge Pl.
Kitchener, Ontario, Canada
N2N 2M7
Phone: (517) 745-1452
E-mail: mbburden@look.ca
www.caoac.on.ca

Federation of American Aquarium Societies
Jane Benes, Secretary
923 Wadsworth Street
Syracuse, NY 13208-2419
Phone: (513) 894-7289
E-mail: jbenes01@yahoo.com
www.gcca.net/faas

Index

Photographs courtesy of:

AquArt, M. Aronowitz, H.R. Axelrod, L. Azoulay, R. Bell, C. Church, Circonia of America, W. Deas, J. Fatherree, R. Fenner, U.E. Friese, B. Gately, M. Gilroy, R. Goemans, J.F. Hemdal, P. Hunt, S. Johnson, G. Lange, O. Lucanus, K. Lucas, R. Mesa, A. Norman, J. O'Malley, M. Paletta, M.P. & C. Piednoir, C. Platt, J. Reyes, G. Schmelzer, Dr. R. Shimek, M. Smith, M. Sweeny, Dr. Z. Takacs, E. Taylor, J. Tyson, M. Walls, R. Wederich, K. Wickstein, and M. Wittenrich